Original title:
Snowlit Woods

Copyright © 2024 Swan Charm
All rights reserved.

Author: Sabrina Sarvik
ISBN HARDBACK: 978-9916-79-537-8
ISBN PAPERBACK: 978-9916-79-538-5
ISBN EBOOK: 978-9916-79-539-2

Beneath the Weight of Glacial Splendor

Silent giants rise so tall,
Encased in ice, they nourish all.
Whispers of ages long since passed,
In their embrace, time holds steadfast.

Beneath the weight, a beauty lies,
Glistening under steel-gray skies.
Reflections spark in frozen streams,
Nature's own, woven in dreams.

The Enchantment of Frosted Branches

Frosty lace on limbs so bare,
Each crystal formed with tender care.
A dance of light, so soft and bright,
Transforms the woods in pure delight.

Glistening whispers in the breeze,
Nature's art, in quiet ease.
Every branch a tale to tell,
Of winter's touch, a magic spell.

Echoing Silence

In the stillness, whispers fade,
Echoes linger, softly laid.
The world is hushed, wrapped in white,
A tranquil peace, a pure delight.

Footsteps crunch on snowy ground,
In the silence, solace found.
Each breath is sharp, yet smooth as air,
In this quiet, worries rare.

Ethereal Patterns in Snow

Falling flakes in perfect grace,
They etch the earth, a soft embrace.
Whorls and swirls in the moonlight's gleam,
Crafting visions, like a dream.

Patterns dance, in fleeting flight,
A tapestry of purest white.
Each tiny flake, unique and free,
A wonder woven silently.

A Tapestry Woven with Chill

The frost weaves patterns, fine and bright,
In the morning's gentle light,
Whispers of winter touch the air,
With elegance found everywhere.

Branches dance in icy lace,
Nature dons a crystal face,
Echoes of silence fill the trees,
Carried softly by the breeze.

Each flake a story, pure and true,
In a world adorned in white and blue,
Here beneath the soaring sky,
Dreams alight as time drifts by.

The quietude wraps all around,
Within this realm, peace can be found,
The tapestry of frost unfolds,
A secret yarn of stories told.

Life holds its breath, the moment still,
In this woven dream, hearts can fill,
With hopes that glimmer, never fade,
In the beauty of the chill cascade.

Under the Shimmering Canopy

Stars flicker softly, skies awake,
Beneath the trees where shadows take,
Whispers of night in a silken breeze,
Nature's magic stirs with ease.

Leaves whisper secrets, old as time,
Crafting a symphony, pure and sublime,
Moonlight drapes a veil of grace,
A gentle touch on every face.

Crickets sing in harmony sweet,
Guiding the night with a rhythmic beat,
While fireflies dance, their lanterns glow,
Painting the dark with their warm show.

Branches sway, a soft embrace,
In this sacred, tranquil space,
Dreamers gather under the stars,
Uniting souls, beneath Venus and Mars.

With every breath, the night unfolds,
A tapestry of stories told,
Under the shimmering canopy wide,
Heartfelt wishes and dreams collide.

Mysterious Footprints on Frostbitten Ground

The morning breaks with whispering chill,
Strange outlines etched on white and still,
Footprints wander, leading away,
Hints of secrets in the fray.

Each mark a tale left behind,
In the cold air, mysteries bind,
Shadows linger where paths crossed,
A journey begun, but at what cost?

The trees stand guard, ancient and wise,
Watching the stories spun under skies,
With every step, the silence deepens,
Nature's breath, the earth it steepens.

Frosted grasses bend and sway,
Worn by travelers, night and day,
In frozen whispers, echoes hum,
Of laughter lost and days gone numb.

But here remains a trace, a sign,
Of moments shared, of hearts entwined,
Mysterious footprints, fading slow,
Revealing paths where dreams can grow.

The Chronicle of Icy Dawns

A dawn breaks softly, icy blue,
With secrets wrapped in morning dew,
Each breath of air, a shimmering song,
In this realm where hearts belong.

Candles of sunlight, flicker and play,
Chasing the shadows of night away,
Nature's canvas, painted bright,
In colors bold, a pure delight.

The chill dances on each blade,
A promise of warmth that won't evade,
Golden rays kiss the frosted land,
As dawn unfolds, hand in hand.

Birds take flight, singing anew,
Heralding a day fresh and true,
A chronicle begins with light,
As shadows fade from the night.

In the stillness, memories blend,
Each icy dawn becomes a friend,
A tapestry woven through time's embrace,
The beauty of life, a sacred space.

Silhouettes Against the Winter Sky

Barren trees stretch towards the light,
Their shapes like shadows in the night.
Cold winds whisper through the pines,
While silence wraps the world in signs.

Frosted fields lie still and bare,
A blanket of white beyond compare.
Clouds drift slowly, gray and wise,
Framing silhouettes 'gainst winter skies.

Stars twinkle faintly in the chill,
The moon, a lantern, watches still.
A magic wraps the frozen night,
As all the world absorbs the light.

Footprints mark the path we wander,
Soft echoes of the dreams we ponder.
Every step disturbs the peace,
In this landscape where we find release.

Hidden Tales of the Icy Realm

Beneath the surface, silence reigns,
Old secrets buried in icy chains.
Whispers of ages lost in snow,
Tales that only the winter knows.

Icicles dangle like frozen tears,
Betraying the passage of fleeting years.
Each glimmer hints at stories untold,
Of hearts once warm, now icy and cold.

In the heart of frost, the truth unfolds,
Memories trapped in the bitter cold.
Nature's canvas, a brilliant sight,
Where shadows dance in pale moonlight.

Ancient echoes linger in the air,
Frosty breath speaks of love and despair.
In every nook and chill embrace,
Lie hidden tales of this frozen place.

Treasures of the Frost-covered Earth

Soft remnants of a vibrant past,
Beneath the frost, treasures hold fast.
Crystals shimmer in the morning sun,
A silent promise of the warmth to come.

Golden leaves, now silver-kissed,
In every corner, beauty persists.
Nature's artistry, a frosted bloom,
Transforming the world into a gem-filled room.

Under the snow, life waits to wake,
In harmony with the choices we make.
Love and kindness, the true delight,
Shimmering brighter in the cold of night.

Each frosty breath a wish set free,
In every spark, a memory.
Hold on to the treasures, don't let them fade,
In the light of winter, dreams are made.

Secrets of the Frozen Grove

In a grove where shadows intertwine,
The secrets of winter softly align.
Branches lace like fingers in prayer,
Breathless beauty fills the cold air.

Beneath the blanket of glistening white,
Life holds close in the wintry night.
Footprints trace stories left behind,
A dance of whispers through the pines.

Frozen streams sing a crystal tune,
Beneath the watchful eye of the moon.
Every glimmer tells of days gone by,
While silence speaks in the sighing sky.

Hidden paths await the brave,
Adventures linger in the cold wave.
With each new dawn, enigma unfurls,
The frozen grove holds treasures and pearls.

The Alchemy of Winter's Breath

Whispers weave through icy air,
Under a blanket, still and fair.
Each flake a tale, soft and pure,
Nature's magic, cold allure.

Trees adorned in crystal light,
Moonbeams dance, a silent sight.
Frozen branches gently sway,
In winter's breath, night meets day.

Crisp echoes fill the morning glow,
Secrets of the frost, aglow.
A world transformed, tranquil, bright,
Wrapped in silence, pure delight.

Stars like diamonds, shine and gleam,
Reflecting on the dreamer's dream.
A tapestry of white unfolds,
In winter's heart, the silence holds.

Every step a crunch, a trace,
In nature's chill, we find our place.
Breath visible in the frosty air,
In the alchemy, we linger there.

Glacial Reveries

Amidst the ice, a world of peace,
Whispers of nature, never cease.
Mountains stand in frozen grace,
In shimmering light, we find our place.

Skies draped in a pastel hue,
Each dawn reveals a scene anew.
Reflections in the glacial stream,
A quiet moment, a waking dream.

Chilled winds carry tales of old,
Of seasons lost and dreams retold.
In the freeze, a warmth we seek,
In glacial reveries, hearts speak.

Pine trees echo with silent sighs,
Caught beneath the endless skies.
Footprints trace where few have been,
In this wonderland, we feel serene.

A breath of frost, a whisper near,
Each icy touch, a heart sincere.
Together in this tranquil scene,
In glacial reveries, we glean.

Frost's Gentle Kiss

The dawn appears with soft embrace,
Frost's gentle kiss on nature's face.
Each blade of grass a crystal wane,
Warming hearts from winter's bane.

Windows glazed and breath a fog,
Whispers wrap the sleepy bog.
In fields of white, the stories flow,
Frosty air, a soft tableau.

Crisp and clear, the world awakes,
In silence deep, the stillness breaks.
A fleeting moment, here we stay,
With frost's gentle kiss, we play.

Cerulean skies, a canvas wide,
In winter's grip, we take a ride.
Velvet nights and sparkling days,
Frost's touch in so many ways.

As shadows fall, stars glint and twine,
Every heart beat, a perfect line.
Underneath the sapphire sky,
Frost's gentle kiss, time slips by.

The Hollow Echo of Winter

Beneath the snow, the earth sleeps deep,
In the chill, the world they keep.
A hollow echo, soft and low,
Where winter whispers, life moves slow.

Frosted trees like spirits stand,
Guardians of this frozen land.
With every gust, a tale unfolds,
Of winter nights and secrets told.

Footfalls silent on the ground,
In the stillness, peace is found.
Frozen moments, captured tight,
In the hollow echo, day meets night.

Crystals twirl in the evening air,
A breath of cold, a fragrance rare.
In the quiet, hear the call,
Winter's song enfolds us all.

As the sun sets behind the peaks,
The world in slumber softly speaks.
In every echo, memories blend,
In winter's heart, we make amends.

Echoes in a Benevolent Chill

Whispers weave through the night,
Softly carried by the breeze,
Gentle touch of winter's light,
In the calm, the heart finds ease.

Frosted air, a tender balm,
Wrapped in stillness, dreams align,
Nature's song, a soothing psalm,
In the quiet, we define.

Moonlit paths and starry skies,
Guide us through this frozen land,
In the silence, hope replies,
Holding tightly, hand in hand.

Softly fall the snowflakes' grace,
Painting white on ancient trees,
Every flake a fleeting trace,
This chill holds our memories.

In the echo of the night,
Benevolence surrounds us here,
In this frozen, pure delight,
Love and laughter draw us near.

The Breath of an Icebound Dream

In the stillness of the frost,
Winds whisper tales of the past,
Every moment, beauty lost,
In this wonder, shadows cast.

Glisten softly on the ground,
Frozen breath of winter's kiss,
In the silence, dreams are found,
Echoes linger in the bliss.

Moonlight dances on the ice,
Reflecting secrets held so dear,
Time stands still, a quiet slice,
Of the world that disappears.

Hushed and soft, the night unfolds,
Wrapped in layers, cold yet warm,
Stories linger, softly told,
In the heart of frozen charm.

Every breath a fleeting chance,
In the chill, we find our way,
Grasping tight this fleeting dance,
In the dream, we choose to stay.

A Tinge of Hushed Wonder

Underneath the silver glow,
Wonder whispers on the night,
In the dark, feelings flow,
Carried gently, pure delight.

A tapestry of white and grey,
Nature breathes a soft embrace,
In the stillness, shadows play,
Captured in this quiet space.

Every star a distant dream,
Glimmers in the frosty air,
Speaking softly, hearts will seam,
In this moment, we are rare.

With each step, the world asleep,
Left behind, the day's refrain,
In the wonder, secrets keep,
As the night begins to wane.

Hushed and still, the air divine,
Tinge of magic fills the scene,
In this space where hearts entwine,
We are lost, yet truly seen.

Radiance in the Frozen Twilight

As the sun dips low and shy,
Twilight's glow sets the world aglow,
Embers of a fading sky,
Whisper tales of love we sow.

In the hush of evening's grasp,
Frosty vines on windowpanes,
Moments linger, hearts will clasp,
In this chill, the love remains.

Cold embrace of twilight's hue,
Filling hearts with lingering light,
Each soft shadow born anew,
Guides us gently through the night.

With the stars above so bright,
We find warmth in frozen dreams,
Radiance holds us ever tight,
In this world, nothing redeems.

So we breathe the icy air,
Feel the magic fill our souls,
Twilight's song, a sweet affair,
In this moment, time consoles.

Glimmers of Hope in the Frost

In the heart of winter's grasp,
Soft whispers of dawn break,
Glimmers dance on icy glass,
Awakening dreams awake.

Buds of life beneath the snow,
Nestled warm and snug inside,
Nature holds a secret glow,
Where every shadow hides.

The sun peeks through weary clouds,
Casting light on silent hues,
Amidst the snowflakes' soft shrouds,
A promise of life renews.

With every breath of thawing air,
Hope rises in painted skies,
Each moment rich and rare,
As winter's chill slowly dies.

Glimmers spark in frosty days,
A beacon for wandering hearts,
Guiding lost ones through the haze,
To brighter paths that spring imparts.

Frosted Petals on Ancient Ground

Amidst the hush of frozen fields,
Frosted petals lay in peace,
Whispers of the past revealed,
In silence, their beauty won't cease.

Crimson blooms with icy crowns,
Rest upon the earth so still,
Nature's art in winter's towns,
A canvas wrought with quiet will.

Beneath the layers, life will thrive,
Roots entwined in earthy beds,
Ancients weep, yet still survive,
Their wisdom in the silence spreads.

As sunbeams kiss the waking ground,
Soft warmth begins to take its hold,
In every crack, new hope is found,
A whispered tale of life retold.

Frosted petals tell their lore,
Of seasons past and lessons learned,
In every flake, a magic store,
As legacy through time is turned.

Nature's Quiet Resilience

In shadows deep, where silence reigns,
Nature stands, unbowed, unchained,
Roots grip tight through stormy strains,
With every challenge, strength is gained.

The trees may bend, but never break,
Their arms stretch wide to touch the sky,
With every howl, no choice but wake,
In every whisper, life won't die.

Gentle streams carve through the rock,
Patient echoes of time flow,
Each pebble turned, each tick of clock,
Resilience molds where winds may blow.

In tender blooms that grasp the mud,
A beauty formed from battles fought,
Amidst the frost and rivers' flood,
Nature's heart remains unbought.

Through seasons' waltz and tempests' hymn,
A story woven, proud and old,
In every crack, a chance to brim,
Nature's quiet strength unfolds.

Treading Lightly through Icebound Dreams

Underneath a starry veil,
Footsteps whisper soft and low,
Heartbeats echo in the pale,
As icy winds begin to blow.

Glistening paths of shimmering frost,
Call the dreamers to explore,
Yet in this beauty, warmth is lost,
Navigating through frozen lore.

Moonlit secrets shimmer bright,
In the quiet, dreams take flight,
With each breath, the world feels right,
In the stillness of the night.

Treading lightly, gentle souls,
Find their way through crystal beams,
With every step, the night unfolds,
Filling minds with vivid dreams.

Delicate chains of fate combine,
Weaving paths through moonlit streams,
In this dance, all hearts align,
Treading softly through icebound dreams.

Frosted Boughs and Quiet Moments

Frosted boughs hang low,
Whispers of winter's breath,
Stillness drapes the world,
In nature's quiet rest.

Snowflakes dance like dreams,
Kissing each branch and stone,
A soft blanket of white,
Where silence calls us home.

Footprints trace a path,
Through the shimmering light,
Each step a gentle pause,
In the heart of the night.

Branches heavy with frost,
Crystals twinkling like stars,
In this moment so sweet,
We find peace, no more wars.

The world slows its pace,
As time starts to dissolve,
In frosted boughs we trust,
Our souls begin to evolve.

A Tapestry of Frozen Dreams

In the hush of the dawn,
Dreams weave through the night,
Cold air breathes softly,
Blanketing all in white.

Each branch a story tells,
In the frost's gentle glow,
Nature's artistry shines,
In the crispness, we know.

Whirls of snowflakes swirl,
Like dancers in the breeze,
A tapestry unfolds,
Crafted with graceful ease.

The sky wears a pale hue,
As shadows start to blend,
Frozen dreams linger on,
Each moment, a rare gem.

Wrapped in winter's embrace,
We find warmth in the cold,
A world of frozen dreams,
In whispers, we are bold.

Luminescent Silence

In the glow of the night,
Silence begins to hum,
Stars wink in the dark,
An orchestra, we come.

The moonbeams softly play,
Across the velvet ground,
A luminescent touch,
Where magic can be found.

Footsteps gently pad,
On frost-kissed, silent leaves,
Each sound a treasured note,
In the symphony that breathes.

Beneath the glow above,
The world feels far away,
In this luminescent peace,
Night turns to a bright day.

Wrapped in silken light,
The shadows hold us tight,
In this moment divine,
We embrace the night.

The Enchanted Glade at Dusk

In the glade where shadows play,
Dusk casts its tender hue,
Whispers float on the breeze,
As stars begin to strew.

Moss blankets the soft ground,
Like a silent embrace,
The enchanted lights twinkle,
In this mystical place.

Trees lean in, secrets shared,
Underneath the glowing moon,
Nature sings in soft tones,
A sweet and tranquil tune.

Fireflies blink with delight,
Guiding lost souls at night,
Their dance a fleeting dream,
In the fading daylight.

In the hush of this glade,
We find a world anew,
Where twilight weaves its magic,
In deep shades of indigo.

Shadows of the Frostbitten Realm

Whispers dance beneath the trees,
In shadows cast by icy breeze.
Frosted branches, silver glow,
Secrets of the night bestow.

Echoes linger, soft and low,
In the realm where moonlight flows.
Chill of winter's breath is near,
Haunting songs for those who hear.

Footsteps crunch on frozen ground,
In this land where dreams are found.
Each shadow tells a silent tale,
Of time suspended, pale and frail.

Glimmers of the stars above,
Whispering the warmth of love.
Yet the winter's grasp is tight,
Holding fast through endless night.

In the quiet, hearts entwine,
Painting warmth in every line.
Though the frost may claim its throne,
In this realm, we are not alone.

Crystal Ferns and Frozen Fables

Amidst the ferns, a tale unfolds,
In crystal forms, the magic holds.
Fables spun from winter's breath,
Whispers of enchantment, life and death.

Frozen leaves in silence gleam,
Echoes of a lost dream's beam.
Every step, a secret shared,
Within the frost, our hearts are bared.

Shimmering jewels on branches sway,
Guiding us through the cold ballet.
Stories etched in ice and snow,
In a world where wonders grow.

Beneath the quiet, life persists,
Hidden truths in shadowed mists.
Frozen fables call our names,
And in this realm, we play our games.

Through crystal ferns, we wander wide,
With hearts aglow and spirits tied.
In frozen realms, our souls ignite,
Luminous within the night.

The Heart of Winter's Court

In the palace of icy dreams,
Crystal chandeliers catch moonbeams.
The heart beats strong in winter's grasp,
Within this realm, emotions clasp.

Whispers slide on frigid air,
Ghostly echoes of hearts laid bare.
Each flake of snow doth softly fall,
A gentle touch, a winter's call.

Shadows flit through halls of white,
Dancing in the pale moonlight.
The warmth within, a secret keep,
As silence cradles those who weep.

In the throne of frost, we stand,
Holding tightly, hand in hand.
The heart of winter's court beats loud,
In solemn vows, we are enshrouded.

Though the chill may carve its ways,
Love endures through twilight days.
In this court, our spirits soar,
As winter's heart forevermore.

Silence Wrapped in a Blanket of White

Silence blankets the world in white,
Hushing all in the soft twilight.
Each flake settles, pure and light,
The calm before the day takes flight.

Beneath the hush, whispers rise,
A symphony of muffled sighs.
Dreams take shape in frosted seams,
Woven softly through moonlit beams.

Trees stand tall, draped in lace,
Nature's hold, a warm embrace.
Every breath is crisp and clear,
As winter wraps its arms near.

In the quiet, hearts find peace,
From the chaos, sweet release.
The world transforms, a timeless sight,
In silence wrapped in a blanket of white.

Through the night, we lose our way,
Yet find ourselves in soft decay.
In winter's arms, we learn to see,
The beauty in tranquility.

A Symphony of Silent Branches

Beneath the whispering leaves,
A melody of soft sighs flows,
Each branch a note in winter's song,
Their silence speaks where no one knows.

In shadows deep and cool embrace,
The breezes dance, a gentle sweep,
While twinkling stars above them gaze,
In harmony with night's sweet sleep.

A secret world of faded dreams,
The woodlands yield their hidden tales,
Through tangled roots and quiet streams,
In every heart a memory sails.

As twilight falls with velvet grace,
The branches brush against the sky,
A symphony that time won't trace,
In silence, here, our spirits fly.

Awash in moonlight's silver gleam,
The night is wrapped in magic's thread,
In every pause, a silent theme,
Where every thought is gently fed.

Footsteps in the Frosted Night

The world adorned in crystal white,
Footsteps crunch beneath the stars,
Each echo soft as whispered prayers,
A journey marked by frost and scars.

Beneath the moon's pale, watchful eye,
Shadows stretch and gently sway,
The chill wraps round like time's embrace,
As dreams and night lend light their play.

With every step, the past unfolds,
Invisible threads weave through the trees,
In solitude, the heart feels gold,
As winter's chill breathes on the breeze.

The air is crisp, as thoughts take flight,
In solitude, the night inspires,
With every breath, my spirit's light,
Through frosted paths, my heart aspires.

With dawn approaching, I retreat,
Each footprint fading in the glow,
Yet memory echoes in the street,
Of frosted nights and whispered snow.

The Elegy of Winter Air

In winter's grasp, the world exhales,
A breath that freezes time in place,
Each gust, a tale of silent trails,
Carried by the chilled embrace.

The barren trees reach skyward tall,
In mourning cloaks of snow and ice,
While echoes of the past may call,
The silence drapes like soft device.

For every flake that twirls and falls,
A story written, weaved in air,
The elegance of nature's thralls,
In frozen verses, caught in stare.

As twilight looms, the shadows grow,
A blanket wraps the land in hush,
While night's still heart begins to glow,
And quiet brings the world to blush.

Yet in this stillness, light remains,
A promise born from starry sight,
In winter's chill, a warmth sustains,
An elegy of soft, pure light.

The Light of Imprisoned Stars

In twilight's grasp, the stars are caught,
Their brilliance trapped in shadows long,
Yet still they pulse with dreams unsought,
A symphony of night's sweet song.

Suspended high, they flicker bright,
A thousand wishes bound and stilled,
Each spark a tale of lost delight,
In fleeting moments, hope is filled.

The moon looks down, a guiding hand,
While whispered secrets float on air,
In yearning hearts, they understand,
The light that shines from dark despair.

With every blink, a story shared,
Of love and loss beneath the night,
In stillness, souls find solace dared,
As hearts ignite in radiant flight.

Imprisoned stars will someday break,
And fill the world with glowing grace,
Through every longing that we make,
Their light will guide us through time's space.

A Canvas of Whispering Frost

In the hush of night, frost gleams bright,
Painting the world in silver light.
Each breath a cloud in the chilly air,
Nature wrapped in a crystal snare.

Trees stand tall in their icy grace,
Adorned in white, they hold their space.
Footsteps crunch on the frozen ground,
Where solitude and silence abound.

Stars twinkle in the velvet sky,
As whispers of winter softly sigh.
A world transformed, so still, so clear,
The magic of frost draws me near.

Frozen streams in a shimmering trance,
Reflecting moonbeams that dance and prance.
In the heart of the night, dreams take flight,
In this canvas of whispering light.

Embracing the chill with open arms,
Winter's breath weaves its timeless charms.
In the create of cold, beauty is found,
A canvas where dreams and frost abound.

The Embrace of Winter's Breath

Softly the snowflakes begin to fall,
Covering the earth in a silvery shawl.
Whispers of winter fill the air,
As nature settles without a care.

Pines wear crowns of frosty white,
Guardians of silence in the quiet night.
Crimson berries peek through the snow,
A splash of color where cold winds blow.

The world is hushed beneath the chill,
Chronicles of winter, calm and still.
Footprints lead to where shadows play,
In the embrace of winter's sway.

Candles flicker in windows aglow,
Casting warmth on the falling snow.
Inside, the hearth keeps the cold at bay,
While outside, frost holds sway.

As night deepens, the moon takes flight,
Bathing the world in soft, silver light.
In winter's embrace, we find our peace,
Where time slows down, and worries cease.

Beneath the Canopy of White

Softly falls the snow tonight,
Blankets drape the world in light.
Whispers echo through the trees,
Dancing gently with the breeze.

Footprints trace a silent path,
Leading to the river's bath.
Twinkling stars begin to shine,
Beneath a sky both pure and fine.

Branches wear a frosty crown,
As the world settles down.
Nature's lullaby will play,
In this peaceful, white ballet.

Shadows cast by moonlit beams,
Guide us through our softer dreams.
Winter's breath, a whispered sigh,
Holds the magic, let it lie.

In the night, we find our peace,
As the chaos starts to cease.
Beneath the canopy of white,
Dreams take flight in endless night.

Rhapsody of the Icebound Realm

Frozen rivers, silent flow,
In this land, the cold winds blow.
Icicles like crystal spears,
Sparkling bright through long cold years.

Whispers from the frostbit air,
Tales of journeys, brave and rare.
Nature weaves a tapestry,
Of winter's song, wild and free.

Snowflakes twirl in ballet's grace,
Covering the earth's warm face.
Echoes clap in icy halls,
Where the beauty gently calls.

Beneath the veils of frigid gold,
Secrets of the heart unfold.
In this realm of winter's dream,
Life is but a quiet theme.

Every step meets frosty ground,
Nature's symphony resounds.
In the heart of this cold space,
We find warmth in winter's embrace.

Fables of the Whispering Pines

In the woods where shadows play,
Whispering pines greet the day.
Stories linger in the air,
Secrets from the earth's own lair.

Breezes carry tales from time,
Of love, loss, and silent rhyme.
Branches sway in gentle dance,
Inviting hearts to take a chance.

Among the needles and the bark,
Echoes dwell where it's dark.
Silhouettes of forgotten dreams,
Swirl beneath the moonlit beams.

Sunshine dapples leaf and loam,
Whispering pines tell of home.
Nature's breath infuses life,
With tales woven through joy and strife.

Listen close to every sigh,
Feel the magic as it flies.
Fables of the whispering trees,
Whispered softly in the breeze.

Shadowed Memories in Winter's Grasp

In the hush of snow-clad night,
Memories fade, yet feel so bright.
Footsteps whisper through the dark,
Echoing tales, a quiet spark.

Frozen breath hangs in the air,
Haunting echoes everywhere.
Shadows dance on frosty ground,
In this winter, love is found.

Through the twilight, dreams take flight,
Carrying whispers in the night.
Ghostly forms, they drift and sway,
In the silence, they will stay.

Each memory, both bitter sweet,
Cradled in the snow's cold sheet.
Time stands still, yet gently moves,
As the heart forever proves.

Snowflakes fall like faded sighs,
Covering the past as it lies.
In this grasp of winter's hand,
We embrace all things unplanned.

The Embrace of Shimmering Tranquility

In quietude, the river flows,
Beneath the stars, a soft glow shows.
The moon reflects on silver waves,
A tranquil heart, the night it saves.

Gentle breezes weave through trees,
Carrying secrets on the breeze.
Whispers of peace in shadows play,
A serenade at end of day.

With every sigh, the world slows down,
In this embrace, no fear to drown.
Each heartbeat syncs with nature's song,
Where we belong, where we belong.

Mountains guard this sacred space,
A timeless dance, a gentle grace.
With every breath, the spirit lifts,
In tranquility, our heart truly gifts.

Here, worries fade like morning mist,
In nature's arms, we cannot resist.
The beauty glows, our souls ignite,
In shimmering peace, we find our light.

Gleaming Whispers in Nature's Choir

In morning dew, the petals gleam,
Nature's voice, a soft-spoken dream.
Birds take flight, their songs arise,
In harmony beneath the skies.

Rustling leaves tell tales of old,
In whispers shared, their secrets told.
The sun breaks through the canopy,
Illuminating what's meant to be.

Soft moss cushions every step,
In this haven, the heart adept.
The symphony of life unfolds,
In vibrant tones, the world beholds.

Rippling streams in steady flow,
Echo laughter where flowers grow.
Each note a gift, each sound unique,
In nature's choir, we find our peak.

As twilight falls, the fireflies dance,
In a world entranced by chance.
The whispers linger in the air,
A melody beyond compare.

Enchantment in the Crystal Stillness

Frozen branches draped in white,
A world transformed in pure delight.
Silent realms where echoes freeze,
In crystal stillness, hearts find ease.

Glistening flakes in twilight's glow,
Each one a star, a tale to show.
Footprints trace a whispered path,
In the realm of cold's soft wrath.

Time stands still in icy grace,
A wondrous spell in this embrace.
With every breath, the air is clear,
In the magic, we draw near.

Beneath the moon's enchanted gaze,
We wander lost in winter's maze.
With each new dawn, the frost will fade,
Yet in our hearts, the peace is laid.

In the warmth of spring's bright embrace,
Memories linger, a gentle trace.
The enchantment held in winter's chill,
Forever blooms in time's sweet will.

Pristine Gardens of Ice

Amidst the stillness, gardens gleam,
A canvas bright, a frozen dream.
Brittle petals kissed by frost,
In silent beauty, warmth is lost.

Crystals weave with the morning light,
Transforming earth in sheer delight.
The air is crisp, the colors fade,
In icy whispers, life is made.

Snowflakes softly dress the ground,
In snow-white robes, a peace profound.
Each branch adorned like precious gold,
In pristine gardens, stories told.

The gentle hush, a lover's song,
In every corner, we belong.
Nature's breath, a quiet sigh,
Through frosty realms, dreams fly high.

As seasons pass, a change will come,
The ice will melt, but still we hum.
In every bloom, a seed of grace,
In pristine gardens, we find our place.

The Melodies of Treetops

Whispers dance in morning light,
Leaves flutter in gentle flight,
Birds sing sweet from high above,
Nature's hymn, a song of love.

Branches sway with playful grace,
In the wind, they find their place,
Rustling softly, secrets shared,
In the canopy, hearts are bared.

Sunlight filters, golden streams,
Casting shadows, weaving dreams,
In this world, serene and free,
Treetops hold their symphony.

Beneath the boughs, we find our peace,
Among the roots, our worries cease,
Nature's choir, a soothing sound,
In the treetops, joy is found.

Where the branches kiss the sky,
In their embrace, we learn to fly,
Melodies echo, sweet and true,
In this realm, we start anew.

Veils of Ice and Light

Morning breaks with crystalline views,
In the air, a spark renews,
Frosted branches catch the glow,
Veils of ice, a silent show.

Whispers swirl in chilly breeze,
Nature's art on frozen trees,
Diamonds gleam in sunlight's kiss,
Moments of enchanting bliss.

Glistening paths where shadows play,
Every step, a winter's ballet,
A world adorned in shimmering hues,
Veils of ice, a dream to muse.

Evening falls with stars ascended,
In this stillness, hearts are mended,
Reflections dance on frosted streams,
Wrapped in warmth of icy dreams.

Underneath the moonlit dome,
In this silence, we find home,
Veils of light, so soft, so bright,
In the night, a pure delight.

Interlude of Frost and Fire

Echoes of winter, crisp and bright,
Frosted ground kissed by soft night,
In the distance, flames will rise,
Warmth and chill beneath the skies.

Embers glow with dancing grace,
Heat that melts the frosty lace,
As two worlds meet in twilight's glow,
Frost and fire begin to flow.

Sparks ignite with crackling sound,
Where the frozen heart is bound,
In the clash of light and dark,
Life awakes with every spark.

In the hush, a time between,
Moments linger, sharp and keen,
Nature's pulse, a fleeting trace,
In the warmth, we find our space.

As the seasons spin and weave,
We find stories to believe,
Interludes of frost and fire,
In their dance, we all aspire.

Patterns on the Frozen Earth

Footprints mark the snowy ground,
Whispers of the past resound,
Patterns carved by time and fate,
On the earth, we contemplate.

Frozen rivers, paths unseen,
Trace the stories in between,
Nature sketches with pure intent,
In the silence, messages sent.

Each flake falls, a story's breath,
Woven closely, life and death,
Beneath the layer, life still thrives,
In the patterns, hope survives.

Moments captured, every size,
In the frost, a world of guise,
Shapes that blend in stark relief,
On this canvas, joy and grief.

As the sun begins to rise,
Painting warmth across the skies,
Patterns shift, and we discern,
In the freeze, our hearts still yearn.

Echoes of Winter's Breath

The whispers of the frost,
Dance softly on the ground.
Each moment feels so lost,
In silence, dreams are found.

The cold wraps around tight,
A blanket woven pure.
Stars shimmer in the night,
Their glow a soft allure.

Soft shadows stretch and groan,
Under the moon's embrace.
Each heart feels not alone,
In this enchanted space.

The world in white adorned,
A canvas sleek and bright.
In breaths of winter, warmed,
We find our fated light.

Frosted breath in the air,
Echoing through the glade.
In these moments we share,
Eternal never-fade.

Shadows of the Flurrying Dance

Beneath the swirling flakes,
The world begins to twirl.
Each whisper softly aches,
In winter's gentle whirl.

Footprints traced in the snow,
Lead paths we cannot see.
Where chilly breezes blow,
The heart feels wild and free.

Branches sway in the night,
Casting shadows so deep.
In silence, pure delight,
As dreams begin to leap.

Flurries swirl, a sweet trance,
Around us, they unite.
In this cold, fleeting dance,
We find warmth in the white.

Each flake a love letter,
From heavens up above.
Their gentle touch, a fetter,
Binding us all in love.

A Canvas of White and Light

Softly shines the first light,
Painting the earth anew.
In hues of silver white,
The world is brightened too.

Each flake, a work of art,
Falls gently from the sky.
Whispers of winter's heart,
As time drifts slowly by.

Crisp air fills up with dreams,
Of warmth that lies ahead.
In light, the vision gleams,
While shadows dance instead.

Blankets draped on the ground,
Cover all with their grace.
A beauty that knows no sound,
In this serene embrace.

Through winter's painted breath,
Life breathes in soft delight.
From dawn till quiet death,
We cherish every sight.

The Stillness Between the Trees

In the hush of deep woods,
Nature holds her sweet breath.
A world wrapped in soft hoods,
Lingers through life and death.

Every branch, a wise tale,
Whispered in quiet tones.
The air holds an old veil,
Where magic finds its homes.

Roots entwined in the earth,
Silent stories unfold.
Each moment claims its worth,
As time gently grows cold.

The light filters through boughs,
Dancing shadows below.
Nature's solemn vows,
In stillness, softly grow.

In this haven of peace,
We find our hearts at rest.
In winter's cold release,
We learn to feel the best.

Twilight's Crystal Veil

The day surrenders to the night,
Colors blend with soft delight.
Stars awaken in the sky,
Whispers of the day goodbye.

The breeze carries tales untold,
In the dusk, a shimmer bold.
Veils of twilight wrap the earth,
Cradling dreams of silent birth.

Shadows stretch across the land,
With a touch of gentle hand.
Night's embrace, a tender sigh,
Sweetest lullaby where we lie.

The world transforms in muted hues,
Among the stars, the heart renews.
In the stillness, moments freeze,
Lost in twilight's tranquil ease.

As time drifts like a feathered wisp,
Each heartbeat slows, a softening lisp.
Under the veil, the spirits dance,
Twilight's magic puts us in a trance.

Shadows Cast by Moonlight

Underneath the silver glow,
Silent whispers softly flow.
Moonlight dances on the ground,
Casting shadows all around.

Trees stand tall in quiet grace,
With their shadows in embrace.
Nature holds its breath tonight,
Lost within the purest light.

The world unveiled, a mystic sight,
Echoes drift, a gentle flight.
In the hush, the heart takes heed,
While the stars fulfill their creed.

Dreams unfurl in shadowed space,
Guided by the moon's soft face.
Every whisper breaks the night,
In the depth of dark delight.

Time suspends in silver beams,
Cradling all our secret dreams.
In moonlit calm, we find our way,
As shadows dance till break of day.

The Dance of Frosted Pines

In the forest, cold winds sigh,
Frosted pines touch the crisp sky.
Every branch, a diamond's sheen,
Nature wears a cloak of green.

Rustling whispers in the air,
Life awakens, unaware.
Silent visitors glide and flow,
In the dance of frost and snow.

Echoed laughter through the trees,
Carried softly by the breeze.
Winter's tune plays sweet and clear,
Frosted pines draw us near.

Underneath the twilight's glow,
Footprints mark where dreams do go.
Nature's breath, both soft and bright,
Guiding us through the starry night.

Every flake, a timeless story,
Whispered softly, full of glory.
In the stillness, hearts align,
Lost within the frosted pines.

Echoes in the Winter Grove

In the grove where silence reigns,
Snowflakes fall like gentle grains.
Echoes dance from tree to tree,
Singing songs of memory.

Winter's breath whispers low,
Telling tales of long ago.
Every branch a story weaves,
Captured in the falling leaves.

Footsteps muffled by the white,
Guided by the pale moonlight.
In this sacred, frozen space,
We embrace the stillness' grace.

Winds of change softly call out,
Filling hearts with joy and doubt.
In the grove, our spirits soar,
Echoes linger, forevermore.

Nature's pulse beats strong and deep,
In the winter's tranquil keep.
Let us wander, ever free,
In the echoes of the trees.

The Quiet Prowess of Winter

Silent snowflakes softly fall,
Blanketing the world in white.
Trees stand tall, in graceful thrall,
Whispers of the cold, a quiet night.

Breath of frost upon the air,
Moonlight glimmers on the ground.
Nature rests, a moment rare,
In winter's arms, serene and sound.

Crimson berries, a splash of cheer,
Amidst the branches, stark and bare.
Winter's chill brings us near,
Gathered close, in warmth to share.

Stars above, a diamond grin,
Twinkling down on frozen streams.
Within the stillness, peace begins,
In winter's hush, we forge our dreams.

As embers glow, the fire's light,
We tell our tales, soft and low.
In winter's grasp, a tranquil sight,
A quiet prowess, wrapped in snow.

Under the Shimmering Canopy

Leaves of gold in sunlight play,
Whispering secrets, old as time.
In the woods, we lose our way,
Nature's dance, a gentle rhyme.

Through the branches, shadows weave,
Patterns soft, a lullaby.
In this haven, we believe,
Underneath the endless sky.

Birds are singing, spirits soar,
Voices blend, a sweet delight.
Every heart feels something more,
Under the canopy, pure and bright.

Sunbeams filter through the green,
Dancing lightly on the ground.
In this moment, we've unseen,
Magic in the silence found.

With each step, the forest sighs,
Breath of life in every form.
Together, we will realize,
The beauty of the world, so warm.

A Poem of Glittering Twilight

Daylight fades, a gentle sigh,
Painting skies in hues of fire.
Stars emerge, one by one, high,
Whispers of dusk inspire desire.

Shadows stretch across the land,
Softly cradling the night ahead.
Nature pauses, hand in hand,
In twilight's arms, we are led.

Crickets chirp, tuning their song,
A serenade to close the day.
In this magic, we feel strong,
Lost in dreams as light fades away.

Horizon glows, a painted sea,
Layered deep in purple tones.
In this moment, we are free,
Where time escapes and softly moans.

Together, we will catch the breeze,
With whispers shared, beneath the stars.
In glittering twilight, our hearts ease,
As night unfolds and the world is ours.

Where Time Holds Its Breath

In quiet corners, moments pause,
Ticking clocks remain subdued.
In this space, we feel the cause,
Of dreams entwined, softly construed.

Footsteps linger on the path,
Echoes of laughter in the air.
In this stillness, we find wrath,
Of fleeting hours, yet we care.

Leaves fall gently, brushed by fate,
Time itself bends to the scene.
In this realm, we contemplate,
What it means to be unseen.

Waves of memories ebb and flow,
Moments woven, thread of light.
In the silence, truth will grow,
Where time holds its breath, pure and bright.

With every heartbeat, we shall find,
A treasure found in endless grace.
In this stillness, hearts aligned,
We discover our sacred place.

Night's Breath on Whispering Branches

In shadows deep, the night did sigh,
While leaves above began to cry.
A gentle hush wrapped all around,
As moonlight danced upon the ground.

The breeze it whispered through the trees,
Carrying tales upon the ease.
A symphony of softest sound,
In nature's heart, pure peace is found.

Stars twinkle bright in velvet skies,
Reflecting dreams where silence lies.
Each rustling leaf, a secret told,
In midnight's arms, a truth to hold.

Beneath the arch of cosmic light,
The world awakes from day to night.
With every breath, a story spun,
In harmony, we become one.

So listen close to night's embrace,
It holds a magic, a sacred space.
In whispers low, the heart will glean,
The beauty found in what's unseen.

Silent Footfalls in the Glade

In morning mist, the wild paths lay,
Where creatures roam and shadows play.
Each step a whisper, soft and light,
In harmony with dawn's new sight.

Beneath the boughs, the silence grows,
Among the ferns, the cool breeze blows.
With every footfall, life abounds,
In this serene world, peace surrounds.

The brook does babble, tales it weaves,
While sunlight dapples through the leaves.
A hidden realm where time stands still,
And all is calm upon the hill.

With every pause, the heart finds grace,
In nature's arms, a warm embrace.
The glade invites with open arms,
To lose ourselves within its charms.

So wander forth on paths untrod,
Embrace the stillness, feel the nod.
In silent footfalls, find your way,
In the glade's heart, let spirit sway.

The Essence of Frigid Beauty

The world adorned in winter's hue,
A canvas white, a dream come true.
Each flake that falls, a crystal bright,
Whispers the magic of the night.

Frosted breath upon the air,
A quiet spell, a moment rare.
The trees stand tall with icy grace,
In nature's chill, find warm embrace.

The silence wraps like a soft shawl,
As shadows stretch and snowflakes fall.
A tranquil scene, a breath held tight,
In frozen beauty, pure delight.

With every step, the crunch, the sound,
In winter's grip, true peace is found.
The essence of a world asleep,
In frigid beauty, dreams run deep.

So let us pause and take it in,
The calm that lies beneath the skin.
For in the stillness, hearts will see,
The magic found in winter's spree.

Lanterns of Light in the Frost

As twilight falls, the lanterns glow,
With flickering flames in the cold night's flow.
They pierce the dusk with radiant cheer,
Guiding lost souls, drawing them near.

The frosty air, so crisp and clear,
Bears whispers of laughter, joy, and cheer.
Each lantern bright, a beacon bold,
Telling stories of warmth when nights are cold.

In every flicker, a dance of light,
Bringing hope to the heart of night.
In their glow, we find our way,
Through paths of dreams where shadows play.

So gather close beneath the stars,
Where lanterns shine like distant cars.
In their warmth, we shed our fright,
Embracing the magic of the night.

With every heartbeat, let us trust,
In lanterns' glow, our dreams are thrust.
Together we'll walk, hand in hand,
Through frosty landscapes, bright and grand.

Frost-kissed Memories

In the stillness of the dawn,
Whispers brush against the trees.
Frost-kissed dreams adorn the lawn,
A quiet spell, the heart agrees.

Footprints trace a tale untold,
Wrapped in blankets of pure white.
Each moment cherished, pure as gold,
A tapestry of joy and light.

Memories linger, soft and bright,
As shadows dance in morning's glow.
The warmth of love, a guiding light,
In winter's arms, we come to know.

Time pauses in this frozen grace,
Echoes of laughter fill the air.
We find our safe and sacred space,
In frosty hugs, we lay our care.

And when the clouds begin to part,
The sun will rise and melt away.
Yet still, I hold you in my heart,
A frosty memory at play.

Glowing Footsteps in the Pines

Through the forest, shadows creep,
Softly glowing in the night.
Footsteps echo, silence deep,
Nature cradles us in light.

Pines stand tall, a watchful guard,
Wrapped in blankets of soft snow.
Every breath, a sacred bard,
Weaving tales that gently flow.

Underneath the silver stars,
Whispers of the past still thrive.
Journeying beyond the scars,
Finding where our dreams arrive.

The moonlight paints a pathway bright,
Guiding us through woods so old.
With every step, a spark ignites,
Stories shared, love's warmth unfolds.

And when we pause to catch our breath,
In the stillness, hearts unite.
In these woods, there's no more death,
Just glowing footsteps in the night.

Reflections of a Winter's Heart

In the mirror of the snow,
A world transformed, so pure, so bright.
Each flake a tale, a dance, a glow,
Reflections in the winter's light.

Beneath the chill, warm fires burn,
Hearts find solace, and dreams take flight.
From icy bounds, we gently learn,
That even cold can feel so right.

Winds whisper secrets through the trees,
Carrying hopes on frozen breath.
As silence wraps us in its ease,
We find joy in winter's depth.

Crystals shimmer, a fleeting sight,
Reminding us of what we hold.
In winter's grasp, hearts take their flight,
The warmth of love, a story told.

And when the thaw begins to show,
Footprints yield to spring's embrace.
Yet winter's heart will always glow,
In every memory, every place.

The Echo of a Frosty Dawn

As dawn breaks with a tender sigh,
Frosty whispers fill the air.
Nature stirs, the world awry,
Beauty lingers everywhere.

Golden beams through crystals shine,
Waking life in soft embrace.
In each glimmer, hope will twine,
The frosty dawn sets forth its grace.

Silent woods, a canvas clear,
With every step, we find our way.
Echoes of laughter, bright and near,
In this moment, we choose to stay.

The chill caresses, bittersweet,
Yet hearts are warmer than the sun.
In frosty beauty, life's heartbeat,
As dawn's embrace has just begun.

With each breath, we weave a spell,
In the stillness, love's refrain.
The echoes of a frost we tell,
In winter's arms, we feel no pain.

Midnight's Crystal Veil

In the hush of night, stars gleam bright,
Whispers of dreams take gentle flight.
Shadows dance on silver snow,
Under the moon's soft, tender glow.

Icicles hang from rooftops' edge,
Nature's beauty in a frosty pledge.
Each breath a cloud in the cold air,
Wrapped in silence, beyond compare.

Footsteps crunch on frozen ground,
In this stillness, peace is found.
Every rustle a secret keeps,
As midnight's magic softly seeps.

Over hills and valleys wide,
In this calm, the heart confides.
Dreams unfold in quiet bliss,
Underneath the stars' sweet kiss.

Time drifts by like falling snow,
In the darkness, feelings grow.
Midnight's veil, a tender sight,
Wrapping all in its soft light.

Songs of the Hoarfrost

On branches draped in icy lace,
Winter's breath leaves a chilly trace.
Each crystal sparkles, soft and bright,
A melody in the pale moonlight.

Nature sings in whispers low,
As the world wears a frosty glow.
Every flake a note divine,
Creating symphonies in line.

Through windy paths, the echoes play,
Tales of night and breaks of day.
Hoarfrost dances, a fleeting sight,
Illuminating the quiet night.

Crisp air carries a haunting tune,
Beneath the watchful, silent moon.
Songs of winter, pure and clear,
Filling hearts with love and cheer.

As dawn approaches, gold unfolds,
Revealing treasures, new and old.
The hoarfrost fades, but echoes stay,
In our memories, they'll always play.

Beneath the Glistening Canopy

Under trees where shadows blend,
Whispers of secrets softly send.
Leaves like diamonds caught in light,
A world transformed in frosty white.

Glistening branches sway and creak,
In the silence, nature speaks.
Beneath the canopy's embrace,
Time slows down, finds its place.

Footprints mark the winter trail,
Stories woven in every gale.
Here, the heart can softly sigh,
As dreams like snowflakes drift and fly.

With every breath, a frosty chill,
Echoes of peace that time can't kill.
Beneath the stars, we come alive,
In this haven, we will thrive.

Moments linger, wrapped in grace,
Beneath the trees, a sacred space.
Nature's wonder, pure and bright,
Holds us close into the night.

The Lullaby of a Chilling Night

In the stillness, winter sighs,
As stars unfold in velvet skies.
A lullaby whispers through the trees,
Carried on soft, frosty breeze.

Moonlight paints the world below,
A tranquil scene, all aglow.
Each flake falls like a gentle dream,
In the darkness, sparkles gleam.

Crickets tune their nightly song,
Filling silence all night long.
Cradled by the chilling air,
The heart finds peace, free of care.

Shadows stretch and blend with night,
In this calm, all feels just right.
Every breath is a fleeting kiss,
Wrapped in the warmth of winter bliss.

As the night drapes its crystal shawl,
Nature's lullaby beckons us all.
Close your eyes, let dreams take flight,
In the embrace of a chilling night.

Gleaming Trails in Frozen Silence

Footprints trace the glistening ground,
Whispers lost, no echo found.
Snowflakes dance on a gentle breeze,
Nature sleeps beneath the trees.

Moonlight paints the night so bright,
Casting shadows, pure delight.
Sapphire skies above us gleam,
Winter's breath, a chilling dream.

A world wrapped tight in frosty lace,
Time stands still in this serene space.
Each step leads to a secret tale,
In this landscape, soft and pale.

Crystals sparkle, stars descend,
In this silence, hearts can mend.
Gazing up, the heavens sigh,
Underneath the starlit sky.

With every glance, the magic grows,
In frozen light, where no one goes.
The night carries a tranquil song,
In this realm, we both belong.

A Labyrinth of White

Endless paths in shades of white,
Twisting shadows under moonlight.
Each step taken, whispers near,
Echoes shimmer, crystal clear.

Icicles hang like frozen dreams,
Caught in webs of silver beams.
Every corner holds a surprise,
In this maze, where magic lies.

Snow drifts shift, a dance so fine,
Guiding us through winter's line.
Lost in wonder, hearts entwine,
In this maze, your hand in mine.

Frozen branches rise and sway,
Marking paths where lost souls stray.
In the hush, a soft refrain,
Calling us back once again.

A world of white, serene and calm,
Wrapped in winter's gentle balm.
Together we will roam and find,
The beauty in this love, unlined.

Chilling Secrets of the Forest

Beneath the boughs, the secrets dwell,
Silent stories, none will tell.
Frozen whispers weave through trees,
Carried softly on the breeze.

Shadows linger, fragile light,
In the woods, a haunting sight.
Where the footprints rarely tread,
Chilling breath of dreams long dead.

Frosted leaves like diamonds bright,
Sparkling under pale moonlight.
Ancient echoes call the brave,
Seeking truths in the still cave.

Softly steps the wandering heart,
In this realm, where dreams depart.
Chilling secrets waiting bare,
In the snow, whispers of despair.

Mysteries in the wooded sigh,
Breathe them in, let your spirit fly.
Among the trees, find your grace,
In the hush of this sacred place.

In the Shade of Icy Boughs

Cool embrace of branches strong,
Where the winter birds belong.
Icy boughs with diamonds hung,
Nature's lullaby is sung.

Sheltered deep from sun's warm rays,
In this haven, time decays.
Frosty fingers touch the ground,
In the quiet, peace is found.

Each breath taken, crisp and clear,
Moments linger, ever near.
In the shade, dreams softly twine,
Cradled in the fated line.

Winter's charm unfolds its grace,
In the shadows, hearts will race.
Embracing chill, we find our way,
In the shade, forever stay.

A sanctuary made of frost,
In this stillness, never lost.
Wrapped in warmth, despite the cold,
In the shade, our love unfolds.

Enchanted Icicles

Glimmering shards hang from the eaves,
A crystal dance, nature's reprieve.
Each drop a story, frozen in time,
Whispering secrets, sublime and prime.

Icicles shimmer in the pale light,
Casting rainbows, a wondrous sight.
Magic weaves through the winter air,
Enchanting the world, beyond compare.

Under the weight of the silent snow,
Icicles drip with a gentle glow.
Nature's jewels in frosty embrace,
Reflecting wonder, a delicate grace.

As winter wanes, they melt away,
Releasing hopes of a brighter day.
Yet in their absence, memories gleam,
Of icy realms that flicker and dream.

Dreams Beneath a Shroud of White

Beneath the snow, the earth lies still,
Wrapped in dreams, a tranquil thrill.
Whispers of life, softly entwined,
In winter's fold, peace we find.

The world transformed, a cloak so pure,
Silent stories, nature's allure.
Footsteps echo in the frosty air,
As hidden wonders await us there.

Stars twinkle down, in velvet skies,
Guiding the night with whispered sighs.
Snowflakes fall like secrets unsaid,
Blanketing dreams, where hearts are led.

In this soft hush, we dare to dream,
Of spring's return, life's vibrant scheme.
Beneath the shroud, hope gently sleeps,
Awaiting the thaw, where the heart leaps.

Winter's Lullaby

Snowflakes drift like whispers near,
A gentle song that we hold dear.
Winter's breath, a soothing chime,
Cradling hearts in perfect rhyme.

The world is hushed, a soft embrace,
As stars peek through, in chilly grace.
Moonlight casts a silver glow,
Upon the landscape, pure and slow.

Nature's choir sings soft and sweet,
In every rustle, a rhythmic beat.
The frosty winds hum low and clear,
A melody, calming, drawing near.

As night unfolds, embrace the quiet,
In winter's lull, there lies a riot.
Each breath a note, each step a tune,
In harmony with the silent moon.

The Mirror of the Frozen Path

A path of glass, in winter's grip,
Reflecting dreams with each small slip.
Footsteps traced on a shimmering slate,
Where moments freeze and time abates.

Around the bend, a world unfolds,
In hues so bright, despite the cold.
Every glance holds a fleeting light,
Captured still in the silver night.

Trees stand tall, draped in white lace,
Guardians watching, holding space.
They whisper tales of what has passed,
In the mirror's gaze, memories cast.

As we wander this sparkling way,
Our hearts reflect in the light of day.
A frozen path, yet warm within,
A journey shared, where dreams begin.

Traces of a Moonlit Path

The moonlight paints the quiet ground,
Soft shadows dance, all around.
Footprints linger, tales untold,
In the night, secrets unfold.

Leaves rustle under ghostly breeze,
Echoes whisper through the trees.
Stars above blink in delight,
Guiding wanderers through the night.

A path of silver, winding slow,
Guided by the lunar glow.
Each step taken, dreams are born,
In the peace of midnight's scorn.

The nightingale's soft song adds grace,
In the darkened, tranquil space.
Every shadow tells a story,
Underneath the moon's sweet glory.

So follow where the night leads you,
To the heart of whispers, deep and true.
Where every trace and fleeting spark,
Illuminates the journey's arc.

Whispers of the Silent Thicket

In the thicket, silence reigns,
A hidden world, where calm remains.
Soft murmurs linger in the air,
Nature's secrets, found with care.

Branches weave a tapestry,
Of vibrant life in harmony.
Petals sigh and crickets sing,
In this refuge, peace takes wing.

Each leaf holds a tale of old,
In shadows deep, mysteries unfold.
The scent of earth, so rich, so sweet,
In whispers soft, the wild birds greet.

Sunbeams filter through the green,
Illuminating spaces unseen.
A quiet place for hearts to dream,
In the thicket's gentle gleam.

To wander here is to be free,
Amongst the roots and ancient trees.
Find solace in the softest sigh,
Where stillness reigns and spirits fly.

The Frost's Gentle Caress

A morning shrouded, crisp and bright,
The frost has kissed the world goodnight.
Its delicate touch, a fleeting grace,
Transforms the earth to a silvery lace.

Upon the grass, a shimmer lies,
Mirroring the pale winter skies.
Each blade adorned with nature's art,
A frozen piece of winter's heart.

The air bites gently at the skin,
Yet warmth blooms softly from within.
Amongst the chill, the world awakes,
As sparkling beauty gently breaks.

Trees wear jackets made of white,
Standing proud in morning light.
The stillness speaks in quiet tones,
In the frost's embrace, we find our own.

With every breath, a cloud ascends,
In this moment, everything mends.
For in the chill, warmth always lies,
In the frost's gentle, sweet reprise.

A Dream of Glacial Light

Beneath the sky, so vast and wide,
A world of ice, a mirrored tide.
Glacial beauty, pure and bright,
Whispers softly in the night.

Each fragment catches starlit beams,
Reflecting our most secret dreams.
In the silence, time stands still,
As nature bends to winter's will.

Cascades of blue like ocean waves,
Hold the stories of ancient graves.
Frozen echoes of tales untold,
In crystal shards of blue and gold.

The air is crisp, the horizon glows,
In this dream of ice, the heart knows.
To wander here is to find rest,
Amongst the beauty, we are blessed.

So take a moment, breathe it in,
Let the glacial dance begin.
In shimmering light, we find our way,
In dreams of ice, we choose to stay.

A Tincture of Winter's Whisper

In the hush of snowflakes gray,
Whispers weave through branches sway.
Silent secrets gently glow,
Nature's breath in frost and snow.

Shadows dance on frozen streams,
Echoes sung in winter dreams.
Frosted air, a crystalline hymn,
Time stands still on a world grown dim.

Moonlight spills on paths so white,
Guiding us through endless night.
A tincture of the coldest air,
Wraps the earth in solace rare.

Glimmers speak in chilly breath,
Tales of life, and also death.
In each flake, a story lies,
Winter's canvas fills our skies.

Beneath the weight of peace profound,
Quiet hearts in stillness found.
A tincture of winter holds sway,
Until warmth returns one day.

Emblems of the Frosted Earth

Emblems carved in icy grace,
On the earth, a wintry face.
Frozen petals, nature's art,
Whispers speak of life's sweet start.

Crystals shimmer in the light,
Painting shadows, day and night.
Every flake, a badge of pride,
On this journey, we abide.

Landscapes wrapped in blankets white,
Silent moments, pure delight.
Emblems of the frosted view,
Life's embrace in shades of blue.

Wind's caress, a muted call,
Nature's fabric, soft and tall.
In this realm, we find our peace,
In the frozen, hearts release.

Through the woods where echoes lie,
Birds take wing in crisp, clear sky.
Emblems of the earth's rebirth,
Glistening bright, a tranquil worth.

The Frostfire's Embrace

In the twilight, shadows blend,
Frostfire dances, light ascends.
Softly crackling, warmth so near,
An embrace that stirs the year.

Glowing embers flicker bright,
Chasing away the birth of night.
Whispers glide on heated breath,
Life awakens from the death.

Snowflakes cling to branches tall,
Nature listens to the call.
The frostfire burns, a gentle flame,
In its heart, we find our name.

Stars emerge in velvet skies,
Reflecting dreams in winter's eyes.
Frostfire's warmth, a cherished bond,
Where every moment lingers fond.

In this realm, both cold and bright,
Together shine, day and night.
The frostfire's embrace we seek,
In its glow, our souls will speak.

Crystal Chains in the Eldritch Wood

In the depths of ancient trees,
Crystal chains sway with the breeze.
Glistening under pale moonlight,
Guardians of the starry night.

Mystic tendrils wrap the ground,
In their thrall, enchantment found.
Every whisper tells a tale,
Of forgotten paths, now pale.

Shadows weave through branches bare,
Secret whispers fill the air.
Crystal chains in tangled vines,
Echo softly, nature aligns.

Footsteps tread on softened leaves,
In this realm, the heart believes.
Magic dwells in every breath,
Softly speaking life and death.

Underneath the starlit sky,
Where the dreams of spirits lie.
Crystal chains in eldritch wood,
Bound by love, and understood.

Whispers of the Frosted Pines

In the hush of winter's breath,
Frosted whispers softly weave,
Between the boughs they trail,
Nature's secrets, hard to leave.

Silent echoes call my name,
As shadows trace the ground,
Pines, like sentinels, remain,
Guardians of the silent sound.

Snowflakes dance in twilight's glow,
A shimmering, gentle lace,
Wrapped in white, the world below,
In winter's soft, embracing space.

Branches bow with gentle weight,
Under crystal's frosty kiss,
Here in nature, still and great,
I find my moment's bliss.

Whispers linger in the air,
A symphony of peace and time,
In the frosted pines, I stare,
Finding solace in each rhyme.

Moonlight on a Silent Trail

Beneath the moon's soft, silver light,
The trail unfolds in shades of gray,
Whispers of the night take flight,
Leading lost souls on their way.

Footsteps merge with gentle dreams,
Nature's breath, a lullaby,
In moonlit silence, beauty seems,
To caress the world, oh so shy.

Shadows form a dancing tune,
As stars twinkle in the sky,
Each bend reveals a silver rune,
Tales of nights that never die.

A quiet path where thoughts can roam,
With every step, a journey starts,
In the light, I find my home,
Mending broken, wandering hearts.

Veiled in night, the moments pass,
Wrapped in magic, soft and pale,
Each heartbeat sings upon the grass,
On this moonlight, silent trail.

Shadows Dance in the Winter Gleam

Where shadows dance in winter's gleam,
A flicker on the frosted ground,
Beneath the stars, a subtle dream,
Whispering secrets all around.

The twilight's chill, a tender kiss,
Clad in velvet, night descends,
Each breath dissolves, a frosty bliss,
As fleeting time in silence bends.

Snowflakes twirl in gentle play,
Crafting art on nature's floor,
In the hush of night, they sway,
Each flake a tale, a whispered lore.

From trees adorned in sparkling white,
To laughter caught in distant sighs,
Shadows dance with pure delight,
Underneath the expansive skies.

In winter's grasp, we lose and find,
A melody of mist and dreams,
With every step, our hearts aligned,
In the shadows' dance, our spirit gleams.

Crystals Underfoot

On pathways lined with icy gems,
Crystals sparkle, bright and clear,
Each step whispers of lost dreams,
In the quiet, we draw near.

Nature's art beneath our feet,
Fragments of the frozen air,
In their beauty, moments meet,
Stories woven everywhere.

As dawn breaks with its gentle hue,
These crystals catch the morning light,
Each shard a memory, sharp and true,
Turning darkness into bright.

With every crunch, a song unfolds,
A symphony of winter's grace,
In the stillness, warmth beholds,
A dance within this frozen place.

Crystals underfoot, we tread,
In the silence, peace we find,
A tapestry our hearts have fed,
In winter's truth, our souls entwined.

The Hush of Glacial Winds

Whispers through the trees, a quiet song,
Nature's breath, where shadows belong.
Cold fingers stretch across the ground,
In the stillness, only peace is found.

Chill across the frozen lake,
A canvas where the memories wake.
Each gust a tale spun from the past,
In the hush, we feel the vast.

Mountains stand with timeless grace,
Wrapped in white, a tender embrace.
The world slows down, holds its breath,
In this moment, we dance with death.

Stars reflect on icy sheets,
Silent night where heartbeats meet.
Echoes of a winter's night,
Wrapped in dreams, so calm, so bright.

Gentle snowflakes start to fall,
A quiet beauty encompasses all.
In the hush of glacial winds,
Life's journey begins and bends.

Frosted Echoes in Still Air

The morning breaks with icy light,
Frosted echoes take to flight.
Each breath a cloud, so crisp, so clear,
In the still air, whispers near.

Branches bear a jeweled load,
Nature's artistry, a frosted road.
Footsteps crunch on snowy floors,
Winter's touch opens hidden doors.

Birds perched still, their songs concealed,
In the hush, a truth revealed.
Silence wrapped in glistening trees,
Tales of winter carried by the breeze.

Golden hues of setting sun,
Mark the end when day is done.
Frosted echoes softly fade,
As night unveils a winter braid.

Underneath the starry dome,
In this stillness, we find our home.
Echoes linger, soft and rare,
Whispered dreams float in the air.

A Ballet of Winter's Grace

Snowflakes waltz on gentle gusts,
Each a dancer, filled with trust.
They twirl and spin in frigid air,
An elegant ballet, beyond compare.

Branches sway in silent tune,
Underneath the watchful moon.
Nature swathes the world in white,
Crafting magic in the night.

Footprints mark a fleeting path,
Whispers of winter in its wrath.
Yet in this dance, we find delight,
Tangled in the soft twilight.

The stillness caresses every heart,
Each note a language of its part.
As stars begin their nightly show,
The ballet weaves a radiant glow.

In the shadows, dreams ignite,
Underneath the velvet light.
A winter's grace, a fleeting chance,
Invites us all to join the dance.

Crystalline Dreams in Twilight

In the dimming light, dreams arise,
Crystalline visions in twilight skies.
Each shimmer tells a tale untold,
Of winter's magic, fierce and bold.

Frozen whispers tell the night,
Sparkling jewels in soft moonlight.
The world transforms beneath our gaze,
Wrapped in winter's frozen haze.

Through the trees, a soft glow spreads,
Illuminating the dreams in our heads.
The air shimmers with secret sighs,
As the day bids a soft goodbye.

Crystalline moments, fleeting and bright,
Carved in ice under the star's light.
In this twilight, we find reprieve,
In every sparkle, we dare to believe.

As night deepens, silence reigns,
Carrying whispers, doused in grains.
Crystalline dreams begin to fade,
Yet in our hearts, they are laid.

When the Earth Slumbers

The sun dips low, the shadows bite,
A gentle hush, in fading light.
The stars awake, a twinkling dream,
As night enfolds in velvet seam.

Crickets sing their softest tune,
Beneath the watchful glowing moon.
The world transforms, a silent sigh,
When day departs and night draws nigh.

The trees stand tall, their whispers soft,
While breezes linger, aloft, aloft.
The earth, it snuggles, deep in rest,
In slumber's arms, it feels the best.

Each creature basks, in peace they stay,
Until the dawn brings back the day.
A tranquil pause, a timeless dance,
In nighttime's grace, we find our chance.

So close your eyes, and drift away,
Embrace the night, don't fear the gray.
For in this quiet, dreams take flight,
When the earth slumbers, all feels right.

Secrets in a Dappled Glow

Amidst the leaves, where shadows play,
A mystic light, a golden ray.
The whispers tell of stories old,
In secrets wrapped, their tales unfold.

The forest breathes with ancient sighs,
While fluttering wings grace azure skies.
Each petal holds a world unknown,
In dappled light, the truth is shown.

A hidden path, inviting glade,
Where echoes dance, and dreams are made.
The air is thick with magic's thread,
In every step, the heart is led.

Beneath the boughs, we wander free,
In nature's lap, just you and me.
The sunlight filters, a soft embrace,
In dappled glow, we find our place.

So hush and listen, close your eyes,
For every breeze, a secret lies.
In nature's arms, the world slows down,
In whispered tales, our joys are found.

Beneath the Stillness of Time

A clock ticks softly, moments creep,
In shadows cast, where dreams are deep.
The world spins slow, a quiet grace,
For time holds secrets, a sacred space.

The river flows, yet never moves,
In stillness found, the heart approves.
With every breath, we drift away,
Where timeless whispers gently play.

The sun may rise, the moon may fall,
Yet time's embrace can feel so small.
In echoing halls of memory's keep,
The past and future intertwine and weep.

Each moment cherished, soft and bright,
Beneath the stars, we find our light.
In fleeting hours, love often gleams,
As we float gently, lost in dreams.

So hold on tight, to what we share,
In stillness' grasp, with tender care.
For beneath the calm, wild hearts can soar,
In timeless love, forevermore.

Phantom Trails in Crystal Light

In twilight's grasp, a shimmer glows,
Through fog and mist, the shadow flows.
Phantom trails weave through the night,
In crystal light, enchantment's flight.

The stars align, a pathway drawn,
To realms unseen, before the dawn.
With every step, the whispers call,
As magic dances, through the hall.

Beneath the veil, reality bends,
As time reveals where wonder ends.
A fleeting glimpse, a world so bright,
In phantom trails, we chase the light.

So take my hand, let's wander far,
In dreams of night, we'll find the star.
For in this moment, we are free,
Lost in the glow, just you and me.

The echoes fade, yet hearts remain,
In crystal light, we break the chain.
With stories told and dreams in flight,
We roam together, through the night.

The Chill of Enchanted Silence

In the stillness soft and deep,
Whispers linger, secrets keep,
Moonlight dances on the ground,
Echoes of a world profound.

Frosted branches, silver bright,
Hold the dreams of endless night,
In this hush where shadows play,
Silence weaves its spell of gray.

Footsteps muffled, gently tread,
Through the realm where thoughts are fed,
Stars above in velvet skies,
Watch as time in stillness flies.

A breath of magic, crisp and clear,
Each sound whispers, drawing near,
The heart beats in soft refrain,
Chilled by beauty, touched by pain.

In this realm, all feels alive,
Where dreams and twilight softly strive,
To capture moments, fleeting, rare,
In the chill, we find a prayer.

Glimmers Beneath the Frost

Glimmers dance on icy sheets,
Nature's paint, where silence meets,
Crystals sparkling in the morn,
Awakening the world reborn.

Underneath the frozen veil,
Whispers of a timeless tale,
Life awakens in the cold,
Stories waiting to be told.

Mornings glisten, hearts ignite,
Dreams emerge in soft twilight,
Each breath rising, misted air,
Hope reborn, a gentle prayer.

Beneath the frost, a pulse remains,
Life's endurance in the veins,
Glimmers shining, bright and clear,
Holding tightly to what's dear.

In the stillness, whispers weave,
Promises that we believe,
In frozen moments, truth is found,
Glimmers glowing all around.

Dappled Light on Icy Trails

Sunlight filters through the trees,
Creating patterns in the freeze,
Dappled light on icy trails,
Guides the wanderer who prevails.

Steps are cautious, breath is slow,
Nature's rhythm, soft and low,
Each footfall echoes in the air,
A sacred dance of silent prayer.

Branches sway with gentle grace,
Time flows softly in this place,
Where shadows play with rays so bright,
Each moment kissed by pure delight.

Frosted grasses shimmer new,
Morning's canvas, painted blue,
Every path, a story spun,
Journey's end yet just begun.

In this world, both cold and warm,
Dappled light does hold its charm,
With every step, heart opens wide,
In icy trails, let love abide.

Enigma of the Hidden Pathways

Twists and turns, a trail obscured,
Whispers caught, the soul assured,
Within the woods where shadows grow,
Secrets pulse, but none shall know.

Paths entwine like tales long spun,
Where light and darkness meet as one,
A maze of options, choices bare,
Each step taken leads somewhere.

Mossy stones in soft embrace,
Guide the wanderer through this space,
With every turn, a question posed,
In silence deep, the heart exposed.

Nature's puzzle, bold and bright,
In the stillness, find the light,
Hidden pathways call and tease,
A journey woven with such ease.

The enigma softly glows,
In the mystery, wisdom flows,
Trust the whispers, feel the sway,
For hidden paths will show the way.

Frosted Serenity

In the quiet morn, still and white,
Frost embraces the ground, so bright.
Whispers of peace, soft and near,
Nature holds her breath, sincere.

Silent shadows dance on the snow,
Each glimmering flake, a gentle glow.
Trees stand tall with icy grace,
A tranquil beauty, a sacred space.

Footprints trace a story untold,
In the frosted world, wonders unfold.
Beneath the hush, the heart finds ease,
Wrapped in winter's tender squeeze.

The world transformed in glacial art,
Nature's canvas, a pure heart.
Moments linger, time stands still,
Frosted serenity, a gentle thrill.

As twilight falls, the stars ignite,
The moonlight dances, pure and bright.
In this stillness, dreams take flight,
Frosted serenity, a soft delight.

Glimmers in the Whispering Pines

Beneath tall trees, the shadows play,
Sunlight filtering, brightening the way.
Whispering breezes tell old tales,
Glimmers of magic, in soft exhales.

Through needles green, the light does weave,
Creating patterns that never leave.
Nature speaks in a hushed refrain,
In every rustle, joy and pain.

Among the trunks, secrets reside,
In the gentle sway, the heart's guide.
With every glance, a story mends,
Glimmers of hope, where the journey bends.

The forest breathes, alive and wise,
In the quiet depths, the spirit flies.
Each step a note in a timeless song,
In whispering pines, we all belong.

As twilight gathers, stars appear,
Shimmering softly, drawing near.
In the night's embrace, dreams commence,
Glimmers in the pines, a true romance.

Nature's Silver Embrace

The moon rises high, a silver dome,
Casting light where the wild things roam.
Nature's arms, open wide,
In her embrace, the world confides.

Gentle streams glisten like stars,
Whispers of night, erasing the scars.
Every leaf a shimmering gem,
Nature wraps us, we are her hem.

Under the twilight, shadows are cast,
Embracing the beauty, the future and past.
In the soft glow, the heart finds peace,
Nature's silver touch offers release.

Mountains rise like sentinels proud,
Beneath the vast, celestial shroud.
In silver light, dreams ebb and flow,
Nature's embrace, a warm afterglow.

The stars twinkle in the velvet night,
Holding secrets, shining so bright.
In their presence, we seek the grace,
Found in nature's silver embrace.

Where the Cold Wind Sings

In the midst of winter's chilly breath,
The cold wind whispers tales of death.
Yet in the hush, a melody swells,
Where the cold wind sings, magic dwells.

Frosted branches sway with ease,
Carrying notes on the freezing breeze.
A symphony woven with silence profound,
In the breath of winter, beauty is found.

The sky hangs heavy with clouds of gray,
Yet hope flickers beneath the fray.
With every gust, the heart knows a truth,
Where the cold wind sings, there's eternal youth.

Through nature's voice, we find release,
In every note, a hint of peace.
The world awakens, though snow may cling,
In the spirit's chorus, the cold wind sings.

As night descends with gentle sighs,
Stars emerge in the velvet skies.
In their twinkle, stories take wing,
Where the cold wind sings, our hearts take spring.

The Luminous Breath of Winter

The moonlight dances on the snow,
Casting shadows soft and slow.
Each breath a spark, a frosty sigh,
Whispers of warmth as time drifts by.

Frost-kissed trees stand tall and bright,
Awash in magic, pure delight.
The chill wraps round like a tender stole,
Painting the night with a gentle roll.

Stars twinkle in the velvet sky,
As winter's lullaby draws nigh.
Nature sleeps in a white cocoon,
Beneath the watchful silver moon.

Each step a crunch on icy ground,
In this stillness, peace is found.
Silent whispers fill the air,
Echoes of dreams without a care.

The dawn will bring a soft embrace,
A touch of warmth, a fleeting grace.
Yet for now, we hold our breath,
In winter's chill, we dance with death.

Whispers of Winter's Embrace

Snowflakes flutter, a gentle kiss,
Nature's canvas, pure and bliss.
Each flake whispers tales untold,
Of winter nights and fireside gold.

The world transforms in quiet grace,
Wrapped in a white, serene embrace.
Branches bow with winter's load,
A secret path, a silent road.

Awake, the owl calls with ease,
Echoing through the frozen trees.
The night wraps tight its shimm'ring sheet,
Where winter's heart and silence meet.

Footsteps muffled, the world at peace,
In winter's arms, all worries cease.
Breath visible in the crisp night air,
Each moment cherished, beyond compare.

With each dawn, the light will glow,
Yet here, the winter winds still blow.
We breathe, we dream, we find our place,
In whispers of winter's soft embrace.

Frosted Silence

In the hush of early morn,
Frosted air, a world reborn.
Crystal sparkles greet the sun,
Nature's pause, time come undone.

Branches glisten, bright and keen,
A radiant, wintery sheen.
Each breath a cloud, a fleeting mist,
In the quiet, we find bliss.

Footprints trace a tale of old,
Stories whispered, secrets told.
The silence sings, a gentle hum,
In frosted air, all hearts succumb.

Embers glow in distant towns,
Softly kissing snowy crowns.
Time hesitates, the world stands still,
In frosted silence, dreams fulfill.

We gather 'round in warmth so bright,
As winter wraps us in its light.
Moments cherished, hearts will sing,
In the frosted silence, love takes wing.

The Stillness Beneath the Canopy

Beneath the boughs, the world is hushed,
In winter's grasp, all life is brushed.
Snow blankets softly, a muffled tone,
In nature's arms, we feel at home.

Silhouettes of trees stand proud,
Wrapped in whispers, like a shroud.
The stillness reigns, a sacred pause,
In the velvet night, we draw our cause.

Footsteps echo, a soft retreat,
In this embrace, we feel complete.
Each breath a promise, each sigh a grace,
The stillness heals, a warm embrace.

Moonbeams filter through the leaves,
Casting dreams where silence weaves.
The world outside drifts further away,
In this stillness, we choose to stay.

With every heartbeat, nature calls,
In the quiet, a soft enthrall.
We find our peace, a tranquil plea,
Beneath the canopy, wild and free.

www.ingramcontent.com/pod-product-compliance
Ingram Content Group UK Ltd.
Pitfield, Milton Keynes, MK11 3LW, UK
UKHW031943151224
452382UK00006B/156